MESSI
SUPERST★R

duopress labs
art by: Jon Stollberg

duopress

First Edition

Library of Congress Catoging-in-Publication Data

Stollberg, Jon.
Messi, Superstar / duopress labs art by: Jon Stollberg. Description: First Edition. |
New York : duopress [2016] |
Includes bibliographical references and index. |
Audience: Age: 9-12. | Audience: Grade: 4 to 6.
Identifiers: LCCN 2015031475 |
ISBN 9781938093579 (Paperback) |
ISBN 9781938093586 (epub) |
ISBN 9781938093593 (Kindle) |
Subjects: LCSH: Messi, Lionel, 1987—Juvenile literature.
Soccer players—Argentina—Biography—Juvenile literature.
Soccer players—Spain—Barcelona—Biography—Juvenile literature. Graphic novels—Juvenile literature. Classification: LCC GV942.7.M398 S76 2016 | DDC 796.334092—dc23
LC record available at http://lccn.loc.gov/2015031475

Printed in China
1 2 3 4 5 6 7 8 9 10 duopress
www.duopressbooks.com

Scan this QR code to learn more about duopress

"When you win a game,
the only thing you can think about is
to win again."

— *Lionel Messi, age 19*

CONTENTS

Chances are that if you are reading this book, you already know who **Lionel Messi** is.

And you probably know that **Messi** is a

SUPERSTAR!!

But do you know **why**
he is such a **superstar**?

Well, that is not an
easy question to answer.

But let's try.

9

"I have never seen anything like him...
the way he dominates games
sets him apart."

— *Javier Mascherano, Messi's teammate with the
Argentinian national team and FC Barcelona*

How can you measure the success of a player?

Individual records & trophies

Comparison with other players

Skill

Commitment

Personality

Passion

Recovery from failure

Let's check out some of these:

Records

Messi has broken many records for both of his teams, Argentina's national team and FC Barcelona.

Other great soccer players have broken many records and received trophies, but **Messi** is really above them all. Let's see why.

Messi has won the **FIFA Ballon d'Or**, the award given to the best soccer player in the world every year, four times. (Ballon d'Or is French for "Golden Ball.")

Messi is the only player in history to win the award four times in a row! That's more than other great soccer superstars like Cristiano Ronaldo, Johan Cruyff, and Michel Platini.

And **Messi** is still young, so he can win the **Ballon d'Or** in the years to come.

Messi wore this polka dot tuxedo the day he received his fourth Ballon d'Or.

"Messi will be the player to win the most Ballons d'Or in history. He will win five, six, seven. He is incomparable."

— *Johan Cruyff, former Dutch professional player and FC Barcelona manager*

Messi — 5 Ballons d'Or

2009   2010   2011   2012   2015

Youngest three-time winner, January 2012 at 24 years old
Only person to win four consecutive Ballon d'Or trophies

Ronaldo — 3 Ballons d'Or

2008   2013   2014

When Cristiano Ronaldo won his three awards, **Messi** was in second place, and when **Messi** won his awards, Ronaldo was in second place. Talk about two competitive dudes!

Messi has been a finalist for the Ballon d'Or seven times in a row, more than any other player in history.

Cruyff — 3 Ballons d'Or

1971 1973 1974

Platini — 3 Ballons d'Or

1983 1984 1985

GOT GOALS?

Here are some records broken by **Messi** when facing the net!

Most goals scored in La Liga (Spanish League)

Lionel Messi
286

Telmo Zarra
251

Most goals scored in a year

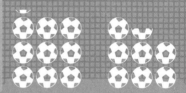

Lionel Messi
91
in 2012

Gerd Müller
79
in 1972

Longest scoring run in La Liga

Lionel Messi
33 goals
in 21 consecutive games

Only top goal scorer and top supplier of assists in the same season

Lionel Messi
50 goals, 15 assists
(2012, FC Barcelona)

Most hat tricks for one team

Lionel Messi   **Cristiano Ronaldo**
27   **26**

First player in Champions League history to score five goals in a single match*

7-1 against Bayer Leverkusen
(*record now shared with Luiz Adriano of Shakhtar Donetsk)

First player in the history of Spanish football to score 40 or more goals in five consecutive seasons

⚽⚽⚽⚽⚽ **47** 2009-10	⚽ ⚽⚽⚽⚽⚽ **60** 2012-13
⚽⚽⚽⚽⚽ **53** 2010-11	⚽⚽⚽⚽ **41** 2013-14
⚽⚽ ⚽⚽⚽⚽⚽ **73** 2011-12	⚽ ⚽⚽⚽⚽⚽ **58** 2014-15

LET'S COMPARE

Greatest Footballers of All-Time

It's hard to come up with a list of the best soccer players in history. But you'll find **Messi** among the greatest players on almost any list.

PELÉ
Brazil

Lionel
MESSI
Argentina

Diego
MARADONA
Argentina

Franz
BECKENBAUER
Germany

Johan
CRYUFF
The Netherlands

Cristiano
RONALDO
Portugal

Zinedine
ZIDANE
France

Let's see how Messi compares with other virtuosos when it comes to what they achieved with their teams.

Pelé (Edson Arantes do Nascimento)—Brazil

Years Played: 21 (*1956 to 1977*)

Clubs: Santos (*Brazil*)
New York Cosmos (*USA*)

National Team: Brazil

Team Titles:
With Brazilian national team:
3 FIFA World Cups

With Club Santos and NY Cosmos:
28 including 2 Copa Libertadores
and 2 Intercontinental Cups

**Total Official
Titles: 40**

Diego Armando Maradona—Argentina

Years Played: 21 (*1976 to 1997*)

Clubs: Argentinos Juniors (*Argentina*), Boca Juniors (*Argentina*), FC Barcelona (*Spain*), Napoli (*Italy*), Sevilla (*Spain*), Newell's Old Boys (*Argentina*), Boca Juniors (*Argentina*)

National Team: Argentina

Team Titles:
With Argentinian national team: 1 FIFA World Cup and 1 FIFA World Youth Championship

With all clubs: 10 including 1 Argentina Primera División, 1 UEFA Cup, and 2 Italian Serie A titles

Total Official Titles: 14

Lionel Messi—Argentina

Years Played: 13 (*2003 to date*)

Clubs: FC Barcelona (*Spain*)

National Team: Argentina

Team Titles: With Argentinian national team: 1 Olympic World Medal and 1 FIFA World Youth Championship

With FC Barcelona: 21 including 7 La Liga Championships (*Spain*), 4 UEFA Champions Leagues, and 2 FIFA Club World Cups

Total Official Titles: 23

**"Messi is a Playstation player.
He makes impossible things possible."**

— *Arsène Wenger, Arsenal F.C. coach*

SKILL

Messi has short, strong legs. (His small stature is actually the reason why he joined FC Barcelona.) Because of this, he is closer to the ground and to the ball than most other players. In other words, he has a low center of gravity. This allows him to turn and dribble very fast. But turning and dribbling fast are not enough. You have to be able to do that while controlling the ball, and **Messi** is a master of that.

Scientists all over the world have studied **Messi's** movements. They have found that when he is dribbling he touches the ball many more times than most players. The frequency of these tiny touches allows him to turn, sprint, stop, and turn again without losing control of the ball, even in very tight spaces. By the time a defender thinks he can steal the ball from him, **Messi** is already shooting at the goal!

Messi can control the ball at close to top speed, but it's his ability to accelerate super quickly that makes him a very dangerous player. Few defenders can keep up with this stop and go, turn, stop, turn again, and go. **Messi** moves and controls the ball like a player in a video game!

Skill and technique are important, but a great player also has to be very smart. **Messi** is an expert at "reading the game." In other words, he can see when to slow down and when to speed up the play, when to pass the ball back to a defender on his team, and when to hold the ball. Sometimes **Messi** gets the ball and stops the play. He looks to the right, looks to the left, and then sends a quick pass to leave a teammate in the perfect position.

Another way to see how smart **Messi** is on the field is when he decides to pull a trick. Of course many players can do tricks, but most of the time they do it for show. When **Messi** pulls a trick or tries a fancy move, he does it because it is the only way to pass a defender or to beat a goalie. He does it to win games.

Secret Weapon

Most players have a dominant foot. That is the foot they use more often to pass, shoot, and dribble. **Messi's** dominant foot is his left, and he scores tons of goals with this weapon. However, since most defenders and goalies know he will try to score with his left foot, **Messi** has trained very hard to improve his shooting and passing with his right foot. And every year he scores more goals with his right foot.

Right-footed goals with FC Barcelona

12 goals *2014–15*	**10 goals** *2009-10*
5 goals *2013–14*	**7 goals** *2008-09*
7 goals *2012–13*	**1 goal** *2007-08*
8 goals *2011–12*	**3 goals** *2006-07*
7 goals *2010–11*	**1 goal** *2005-06*

the head?

Lionel Messi scored a beautiful header to win the UEFA Champions League with Barcelona against Manchester United (England) in 2009. **Messi** doesn't have to be the tallest player to score a header. But he has to have the brains to get to the right spot at the right time!

Commitment

Soccer players, especially the good ones, are busy people. Since **Messi** plays for a top club in Spain and also for Argentina's prestigious national team, it seems that he is playing soccer all the time.

In 2014, **Messi** played 53 games in 4 different tournaments. That is more than a game every week, and this doesn't include friendlies or long and hard training sessions.

La Liga

Copa del Rey

UEFA Champions League

FIFA World Cup

in Brazil

Games Played: 32 + 5 + 13 + 3 = 53

It is fair to say that players like **Messi** spend half of the year on the field and the other half on a plane.

With all these games, players like **Messi** get very little vacation between seasons. But when he does get a vacation, **Messi** is always one of the first to come back to train. Sometimes he even cuts his vacation short to start training before anybody else.

In other words, to become who he is, **Lionel Messi** has had to work really hard. And he does, every day.

Personality

May 2015: FC Barcelona was playing against Cordoba in La Liga. The Barcelona players were having an easy game, and **Messi** had already scored two goals. With five minutes left in the match the referee conceded a penalty to Barcelona. **Messi** was the official penalty taker for the team, and this was a great opportunity to score yet another hat trick. Even more important, **Messi** was head-to-head with his rival, Cristiano Ronaldo, for the trophy for the top scorer in Spain, as well as the Golden Boot, the award for the player with the most goals in all European competitions. The season was almost finished, and one goal could be the difference between these two great players.

As expected, **Messi** grabbed the ball. But instead of placing it in the penalty spot, he gave it to his teammate, the Brazilian star Neymar Jr., who had had a couple of great chances in the game but had not scored. Neymar Jr. scored and gave a big hug to **Messi** after the celebration.

In 2010, **Messi** became the youngest player to score 100 goals with FC Barcelona. At age 23, he was already a superstar and everybody was talking about his talent and great skills. But that's not **Messi's** secret. Joaquim Rifé, one of **Messi's** first coaches when he arrived at Barcelona as a kid, has said that **Messi's** secret is his personality.

> **"Since he was really young, Leo was always a team player who wasn't looking for trouble with anybody. His main talent is that fame has not changed him. He is one of the best players in the world and yet he always puts the team first."**

"I prefer to win titles with the team ahead of individual awards. I'm more worried about being a good person than being the best football player in the world."

— *Lionel Messi*

Imagine that your job is to play soccer. You are really good at it, and you win a lot of trophies and break a lot of records. You are famous all over the world and make a lot of money. Kids from Africa to China to the United States wear jerseys with your name on the back, and fans of every team know who you are and admire you. Sounds like fun, right? It could be a fantastic life. But it is also a lot of pressure. All your fans want to meet you, and whole countries want you to succeed or to fail, depending on where you play. Your coaches want more trophies, and perhaps you want more records. How do you keep up with all this?

One word:

Passion

Passion means to have a strong desire or enthusiasm for something. Like most successful soccer players and other top athletes, **Messi** has a big passion for what he does. **Messi** never forgets the joy of the game. Without that passion and the excitement of kicking the ball around, the way **Messi** has done since he was a little kid, being a professional soccer player and a global star could become very boring.

"I have fun, like a kid playing soccer in the street. If the day comes when I stop having fun, I'm going to quit."

— *Lionel Messi*

Setbacks

Like everybody else, **Messi** has had some tough times. Believe it or not, he has had his share of failures. Let's talk about one. Many people in Argentina, where **Messi** was born, gave him a hard time because he played for Barcelona. However, when **Messi** was called to play for Argentina's national football team (at the age of just 17!), people in his home country cheered. Everybody there was looking forward to seeing the future superstar dressed in the shades of the albiceleste, the sky-blue and white colors of the team.

Argentina was playing a friendly against Hungary. In the 65th minute of the match, **Lionel Andrés Messi** came out of the bench. Everybody in Argentina set their eyes on the substitute. Could this kid be their next soccer hero?

The whole thing lasted 47 seconds. When **Messi** got the ball he quickly dribbled a Hungarian defender. The defender grabbed **Messi's** shirt. **Messi** lifted his arm and tried to get away from him. The referee believed **Messi** elbowed his opponent. He called a foul and showed **Messi** a red card. He was out of the game less than a minute after coming onto the pitch. Everybody thought the referee's decision was excessive. The teenager left the field in tears.

Failure is part of life, and **Messi** would come back from that incident in a very strong way. Argentinian fans adore **Messi** now, and he has said publicly that his dream is to win the World Cup for the country where he was born.

MESSI Quiz #1

Test your knowledge about **Messi**.

In the 2014–15 season, **Messi** scored 56 goals with FC Barcelona.

Goals from headers	**6**
Right-footed goals	**17**
Left-footed goals	**33**

Can you guess how many of these goals came from free kicks?

a) 2
b) 15
c) 7

Find the answer on page 137

GROWING
UP

Fútbol Central

Lionel Messi was born in Rosario, Argentina.

Argentina is located in South America, a continent that has some of the most impressive soccer teams and players in the world.

Rosario

BRAZIL

URUGUAY

ARGENTINA

Just look and see...

World Cup Winners

Brazil

⚽ ⚽ ⚽ ⚽ ⚽ ⚽
Finals Played

Finals Won

Argentina

⚽ ⚽ ⚽ ⚽ ⚽
Finals Played

Finals Won

Uruguay

⚽ ⚽
Finals Played

Finals Won

Famous South American Players

Pelé *(Brazil)*
Ronaldo *(Brazil)*
Ronaldinho *(Brazil)*
Zico *(Brazil)*
Garrincha *(Brazil)*
Enzo Francescoli *(Uruguay)*
Lionel Messi *(Argentina)*
Diego Maradona *(Argentina)*
Alfredo Di Stéfano *(Argentina/Colombia/Spain)*
Gabriel Batistuta *(Argentina)*
Mario Kempes *(Argentina)*

Lionel Andrés Messi was born on June 24, 1987, in Rosario, the third largest city in Argentina. His parents, Jorge Messi and Celia Cuccittini, were simple working-class people. They never imagined how their lives would change after the birth of their third child. **Leo**, as his family calls him, has two older brothers, Rodrigo (seven years older) and Matias (five years older), and a younger sister, Marisol (six years younger). As expected in an Argentinian family, especially one with three boys, soccer was a big part of their lives. Jorge Messi was a huge soccer fan, and Rodrigo went on to play as a striker for a second division team in Argentina. Little **Leo**, though, was not very interested in soccer. As a little kid he loved to play with marbles.

When **Leo** turned four, his parents surprised him with a little white soccer ball with red diamonds. It was a great present, but **Leo** decided to keep playing with his marbles. He had won mountains of them from his playmates.

One day, **Leo** decided to give soccer a try. As often happened in the Messi family, **Leo's** father and his two brothers were playing a game of soccer in the street. This time, **Leo** left his marbles behind and joined the game. He had never played before, but it was clear that he had a knack for soccer. His father and older brothers were shocked by the ability of the little four-year-old.

From that day on, **Lionel Messi** and his soccer ball became best friends.

"We were shocked to see how good he was. And he'd never played before!"

—Jorge Messi,
Lionel Messi's father

Leo's grandmother, Celia, took care of him while his parents were at work. Grandma Celia was also a big soccer fan. She would take the older boys to soccer practice, and **Leo** often tagged along. One day, one of the teams with older boys was short a player, and **Leo** was enlisted to fill in. Some say it was the coach's idea, while others say it was Grandma Celia's. Either way, both worried that **Leo** was too small to play with the other boys.

The coach and Celia made a deal. **Leo** would play near the sideline, close to the coach. If things looked bad or dangerous, the coach would stop the game and take him out.

Leo put on the team shirt. When the first ball came to him, he did nothing. When another ball came, it landed next to his left foot. And that changed everything. This is how Salvador Aparicio, the coach, remembers the moment: "The kid latched into the ball and went past one guy, then another, and another. I was yelling at him: 'Kick it, kick it.' I was worried somebody would hurt him but he kept going and going—I had never seen anything like this. That kid is never coming off the field."

"Pass the ball! Pass the ball to the little guy!!!"

— Messi's grandmother, Celia, shouting from the sidelines in Messi's first match

Leo and his grandmother Celia were very close. Not only did she take him to his first soccer practice, but she was always very supportive. **Leo** was very sad when she died in 1998. Since then, **Messi** honors her memory by raising his fingers to the sky every time he scores a goal.

Shortly after **Leo's** first taste of the soccer field, he started playing for Grandoli, a small club coached by his dad. When he was eight years old, he joined the youth team of Newell's Old Boys, one of the two local soccer teams in Rosario. At Newell's, **Leo** was part of a team that lost only one game in four years. They were known as "the Machine of '87" since all the boys on the team were born in 1987.

At 11 years old, **Leo** was already a famous player on Newell's youth team, and local papers wrote many articles praising the "Next Pelé" or the "New Maradona." But there was one problem: **Leo** was by far the smallest boy his age, and he was not growing at the same pace as other kids. The doctors told his family that **Leo** had a growth-hormone deficiency. His body, in other words, was not making the substance that helps cells and other parts of the body to grow.

Leo needed a special hormone injection every day so he could grow to his full height. **Leo** hated the shots, but he knew he had to do it. There was another problem: The shots were very expensive, and after a couple of years his family couldn't afford them any longer. The Newell's Old Boys organization understood **Leo's** potential and offered to pay for the treatments. Soon, however, the economy in Argentina declined and Newell's Old Boys started missing the payments.

Jorge Messi knew how important this treatment was for **Leo's** life, not to mention for his dreams of becoming a professional soccer player. So Jorge looked for other options, first in Argentina with team River Plate and then with FC Barcelona in Spain.

"Something deep in my character allows me to take the hits and get on with trying to win."

— *Lionel Messi*

MESSI Quiz #2

Test your knowledge about **Messi**.

32 = Record number of hat tricks that **Messi** has scored with FC Barcelona.
But what in the world is a hat trick?

a) When a player controls the ball with his head, as if wearing a hat, and runs down the field

b) When a player surprises the other team by wearing a hat during a corner kick

c) When a player scores three goals in one game

d) When a player runs to the stands and takes a hat from a fan of the opposite team

e) When a player hits the crossbar three times during a game

Find the answer on page 137

3

LEO MESSI: GENIO INSACIABLE

MORE THAN
A SOCCER
SCHOOL

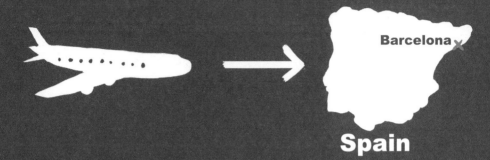

Barcelona

Spain

On September 16, 2000, **Lionel** and his father got on a plane to Barcelona, the second largest city in Spain and home of one of the best teams in world soccer: Football Club Barcelona, or FC Barcelona.

FC Barcelona's motto is "More than a club," and it really is a gigantic organization with three professional soccer teams (first team, Barça B, and Under 18 A); 18 youth soccer teams for boys and girls; and four professional teams in other sports, such as basketball, handball, roller hockey, and indoor soccer. They also have one of the best soccer youth academies. Known as La Masia, this would be **Messi's** next soccer school.

But first he needed to show them how good he really was.

How good is La Masia?

Well, consider this:

In 2010, La Masia became the first youth academy to have trained all three finalists of the Ballon d'Or in the same year. All three players were from FC Barcelona:

Andrés Iniesta

Lionel Messi

Xavi Hernández

When Spain won the 2010 World Cup, the team had nine players from La Masia, including:

Sergio Busquets
Cesc Fàbregas
Gerard Piqué
Pedro
Xavi Hernández
Andrés Iniesta (He scored the winning goal of the final match!)
Gerard Piqué

Pep Guardiola, the famous player and coach, is also a product of La Masia.

Player

Barça
6 La Liga Championships
1 UEFA Champions League

Spain
Silver Medal in the 1992 Olympic Games

Coach

Barça
3 La Liga Championships
2 UEFA Champions League titles
2 FIFA World Club Cups

Bayern Munich
2 Bundesliga championships
1 FIFA World Club Cup

Tryout

Youth coaches from FC Barcelona had seen videos of little **Lionel** playing in Argentina, showing his skills, moves, and ball control. One particular video of **Lionel** started circulating. In the video, coaches could see **Lionel** juggling oranges (or maybe tennis balls) with the same skill that professional players juggle real soccer balls.

But the real test came when **Lionel** had to play in front of FC Barcelona coaches in a game with players who were already accepted and playing in La Masia. It was a difficult challenge but one that any aspiring soccer player has to experience. That day, though, things were a bit harder since all the other players were one or two years older than **Lionel Messi**.

"The only time that I have felt really nervous was during that tryout game with Barcelona."

— *Lionel Messi*

The game had started, and Carles Rexach, the technical director of soccer operations for FC Barcelona, was a few minutes late. Other youth coaches were already impressed with what **Lionel** was showing on the field, but it was Rexach who would make the decision to accept **Lionel** or not. As Rexach walked around the field to get to the bench, he could see that **Lionel** was different from other players. He was small but very confident, agile, fast, and good at running and dribbling with the ball. By the time Rexach sat on the bench he had made a decision. He turned to the other coaches and said:

"We have to sign him. now!"

Normally a new player would train with the youth teams for a few weeks and play a few games before the coaches would make up their minds. Not with **Lionel**. It took him seven minutes to show them that he was ready for FC Barcelona.

However, things were°not that easy.

Argentina

Lionel and his father flew back to Argentina. The entire family was happy and confident that Barcelona would soon invite **Lionel** back and sign the contract that would make him an official FC Barcelona player. But in Europe, some Barcelona coaches were not convinced that signing **Lionel** was such a great idea. There was no doubt **Lionel** was a fantastic player, but he was only 13 years old and had a growth problem that needed a special treatment. There was no guarantee he would develop to become a good soccer player later on. A few months passed and no contract had been sent. **Lionel** and his family were worried.

Lionel's agents met with Carles Rexach in a restaurant in Barcelona and explained that **Lionel** and his family needed to see a contract soon. They argued that Barcelona's rival, Real Madrid, was also showing interest in **Lionel**. Rexach didn't want to miss the chance to sign **Lionel**, so he grabbed a paper napkin, drew up a contract, and signed it. That piece of paper made **Lionel Messi** an official FC Barcelona player.

Of course signing a contract on a paper napkin is not a normal way to sign a player, but Rexach knew that **Lionel Messi** was not a normal player. And he was right.

Soccer teams can't sign a contract with a player, or pay them any money, until they are 16 years old. So, the "contract" that **Lionel** got was in reality a grant, or a scholarship. FC Barcelona offered to pay for an apartment for **Lionel's** family; a position in the club for his father; and school, training, and the growth hormone treatment for **Lionel**.

Lionel's family landed in Barcelona on February 15, 2001. This is what **Lionel** had wanted all his life, but that didn't stop him from crying during the entire flight. He knew his life was about to change forever.

La Masia

Being selected for La Masia doesn't guarantee success. Only one out of ten of the young players in La Masia gets to play on FC Barcelona's first team, and only a few of those become regular starters for the club. La Masia is also a lot of work, and that doesn't necessarily mean just fun soccer footwork. Players who live at La Masia play surprisingly little soccer each day—just over one and a half hours. The rest is schoolwork. Yes. School. Homework. Tutors. Reading and math. You know, all that exciting stuff.

This is because La Masia doesn't want players who are only athletic and good at sports. They want players who are good at thinking and good at making decisions, and who also have good skill and technique. **Lionel Messi** was perfect for this. However, for the first time in his life scoring lots of goals wasn't enough. **Lionel** also needed to get good grades.

Wake up : 6:45 AM
Breakfast : 7:00 AM
School Bus Pickup: 7:00 AM
School : 7:30 AM
Lunch + Free Time: 8:00 AM - 2:00 PM
Training : 2:00 - 4:00 PM
Showers : 4:00 - 6:00 PM
Tutoring/Homework: 6:00 PM
Dinner : 6:30 - 8:30 PM
TV/Internet: 9:00 PM
Bedtime: 10:00 - 11:00 PM
11:00 PM

Soccer in La Masia is taught in the particular style of play of FC Barcelona. Everybody, from the very young kids to the first squad players, practices under the same ideas:

1 Everybody has to work together—teamwork and collaboration are key.

2 When the team doesn't have the ball, all players put pressure on the ball as quickly as possible.

3 When the team gets the ball, it keeps it as much as possible; this is called ball possession.

4 Passing the ball around to other teammates has to be done fast and with pinpoint accuracy.

5 Attack with as many players as possible.

For **Lionel**, all this focus on teamwork was new. Back in Argentina he would do everything himself!

La Masia is not the only famous soccer academy. Here are some other celebrated schools of soccer and some of the players who played there:

AFC Ajax
(Netherlands)
Clarence Seedorf

Real Madrid CF
(Spain)
Raúl
Emilio Butragueño

Sporting Libson
(Portugal)
Cristiano Ronaldo

Manchester United FC
(England)
David Beckham
Ryan Giggs

Santos FC
(Brazil)
Neymar Jr.
Pelé

FC Bayern Munich
(Germany)
Philipp Lahm
Toni Kroos

"I have seen the player who will inherit my place in Argentinian football and his name is Messi."

— *Diego Maradona on the 18-year-old Messi, February 2006*

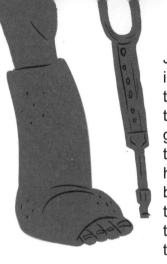

Just wearing the FC Barcelona jersey, of course, is not enough, and early on **Lionel** struggled to adapt to his new team's style of play. And then there were the injuries. In his second game after arriving in Barcelona, **Lionel** tried to stop an opposing player who was about to hit a volley and broke his fibula (one of the two bones between the knee and ankle). To make things worse, when he finally recovered from that injury, he fell down the stairs and strained the ligaments in his right ankle.

In four months, **Lionel** played two games, scored one goal, and got injured twice.

Argentina

The family flew back to Argentina for a few days. **Lionel** needed to make a decision. It was clear that he was too small and fragile. Things in Barcelona were much harder than expected.

But did he quit?

"I was a striker, but Leo has something I never had: He is so determined, he has worked so hard and has made so many sacrifices to become who he is today."

— *Rodrigo Messi, Lionel's brother*

Not a chance. **Lionel** returned to La Masia and began to build a reputation on Barcelona's youth teams. The hormone treatment was working, and he was growing again. However, he was still shorter than most players and was often called La Pulga, or "the Flea." And he wasn't free of injuries (once, a defender broke **Lionel's** jaw in a header).

But that didn't matter; **Lionel** became more comfortable with the style of play in La Masia and found his place on the team. He moved up quickly from category to category, scoring tons of goals along the way.

37 goals in 30 matches with FC Barcelona Cadet A
2003

1 goal in 1 match with FC Barcelona Youth B
2004

21 goals in 14 matches with FC Barcelona Youth A
2004

He had a taste of FC Barcelona's first team during a friendly game against Porto of Portugal in 2003. Although this was a dream come true for the 16-year-old **Lionel**, it was only the beginning. In a few months, he would be called to defend the blaugrana (blue and red) colors of FC Barcelona in an official game for the first time.

MESSI Quiz #3

Test your knowledge about **Messi**.

The traditional colors of FC Barcelona's jersey are blue and red vertical stripes. But the day **Lionel** played his first game with Barcelona's first team, in a friendly against Porto, the team wore a not-very-traditional kit. Do you know which color they wore that day?

a) Brownish color, with two horizontal stripes, one red, one blue

b) Bright yellow

c) Red and blue horizontal stripes

d) White shirt with two horizontal stripes, one red, one blue

Find the answer on page 137

FC BARCELONA

"GOOOOOOAL!

Goal, goal, goal!"

"Goal, goal, gooooooooooal...historic goal by Leo Messi! 252 goals! He is the best player; he is the best scorer in La Liga history. A goal for the history books!"

This is how a Spanish TV announcer called the moment in which **Messi** became the best scorer in La Liga history, on November 22, 2014, at Barcelona's Camp Nou stadium. The old record, by Telmo Zarra, a famous Spanish striker, had been unbeaten for almost 60 years. And **Messi** had done it in only 11 seasons, four less than Zarra.

After **Messi** scored the record-breaking goal, the entire stadium chanted his name and his teammates lifted him in celebration. It took only a few minutes for **Messi** to score another goal, and he went on to end the game with a hat trick.

The question everybody is asking today is how many more goals can **Messi** score? After all, he still has more years to play. Can he double the number of goals Zarra scored? Is that even possible? Only time will tell.

But one thing is clear: **Messi's** decision to join FC Barcelona was the best of his career. And of course the same goes for FC Barcelona. The small kid from Argentina has become the biggest star in the history of the team.

FC Barcelona was founded in 1899 when a group of players invited by Joan Gamper, a Swiss immigrant, got together to form a team. Today, Barça, as it's familiarly known, is one of the most successful sports teams in the world with millions of supporters and followers on social media. Barça is a bit like a democratic country. The team is actually owned and run by its fans. They can vote for the team's president and other issues, just like citizens vote to elect their leaders in a country.

Top 10 All-Time Barcelona Players

Carles Puyol
Defender (Spain)

Andoni Zubizarreta
Goalie (Spain)

Andrés Iniesta
Attacking Midfielder (Spain)

Pep Guardiola
Midfielder (Spain)

Johan Cruyff
Attacking Midfielder (Netherlands)

Xavi
Midfielder (Spain)

Rivaldo
Forward (Brazil)

Samuel Eto'o
Striker (Cameroon)

Ronaldinho
Forward (Brazil)

Lionel Messi
Attacking Midfielder, Forward (Argentina)

Like other big European soccer teams, FC Barcelona competes in many tournaments during the year. Some of these are local competitions in Spain, such as La Liga or Copa del Rey. Others are regional tournaments, where the best teams on the continent play each other in cups like UEFA Champions League or Europa League. And there is also a FIFA Club World Cup.

El Clásico

Faces the two biggest teams in Spain against each other:
FC Barcelona vs Real Madrid

El Derbi Barceloní

The two teams in the city face each other:
FC Barcelona vs RCD Espanyol

"El Clásico between Barça and Real Madrid, and Argentina vs Brazil are two of the biggest games in the world. Not just for the players but also the fans."

— *Lionel Messi*

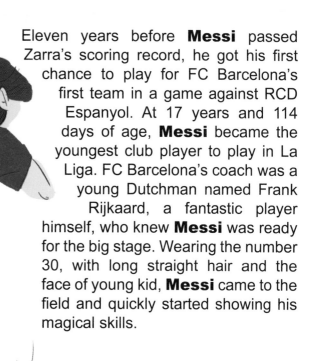

Eleven years before **Messi** passed Zarra's scoring record, he got his first chance to play for FC Barcelona's first team in a game against RCD Espanyol. At 17 years and 114 days of age, **Messi** became the youngest club player to play in La Liga. FC Barcelona's coach was a young Dutchman named Frank Rijkaard, a fantastic player himself, who knew **Messi** was ready for the big stage. Wearing the number 30, with long straight hair and the face of young kid, **Messi** came to the field and quickly started showing his magical skills.

His first goal came a few weeks later, when he scored the same goal twice. This is what happened: FC Barcelona was winning a game against Albacete, and Coach Rijkaard called **Messi** out from the bench. A few minutes into the game, **Messi** and Brazilian superstar Ronaldinho connected in a beautiful pass. **Messi** flicked the ball over the goalie and scored! But the referee thought **Messi** was offside, and the goal didn't count. Only a few minutes later, **Messi** and Ronaldinho connected again, in what looked like a copy of their last play. Again, **Messi** flicked the ball over the goalie and scored. This time it counted.

Ronaldinho   **Messi**   **Goalie**

"Soccer should make people happy and that's what Messi does. He makes people happy."

— *Frank Rijkaard, Barcelona coach 2003-2008*

In the next couple of seasons **Messi** became a regular on Barcelona's first team. However, as had happened in his first years at La Masia, **Messi** got injured twice and missed many important games. By March 2007, he returned to his best form by scoring a hat trick against archrivals Real Madrid in El Clásico. This was an epic performance against the biggest and most-despised Barcelona rival in La Liga. At 19 years old, an age at which most players are dreaming of their first opportunity on the field, **Lionel Messi** had already become a legend of FC Barcelona.

Barcelona Top Ten Club Achievements After Lionel Messi Joined the Team

2009—Barcelona becomes the first Spanish club to win the European continental treble (three trophies in one year) by winning La Liga, Copa del Rey, and the UEFA Champions League.

2009—Barcelona becomes the first to win the sextuple by winning six competitions out of six in one year: La Liga, Copa del Rey, UEFA Champions League, Spanish Super Cup, UEFA Super Cup, and FIFA Club World Cup.

14 trophies in four years (2008 to 2011) under coach Pep Guardiola

2015—Barcelona becomes the first European club in history to achieve the continental treble twice.

7
La Liga titles

4
*UEFA Champions
League titles*

3
Spanish Cup titles

2
*UEFA Super
Cup titles*

6
*Spanish Super
Cup titles*

2
*FIFA Club
World Cup titles*

Barça Partners and Buddies

Soccer is a team sport; good teammates make you a better player, and great ones make you even better! On FC Barcelona, Messi has been fortunate to play alongside some fantastic players and coaches.

Ronaldinho

The Brazilian star Ronaldinho was Messi's first partner on the team. Together they marveled fans around the world with their skill and communication on the field. When Ronaldinho left Barça, he passed Messi the iconic number 10 that has adorned his shirt ever since.

Pep Guardiola

Former Barcelona player-turned-coach Pep Guardiola decided that Messi should leave the position of right winger (along the sideline) and play in what he called a "false 9" or false striker. This move put Messi in the center of the front line, like a striker but with much more freedom to move around the pitch. Messi and Barcelona exploded with Guardiola's coaching, winning 14 titles in four years!

"We are witnessing the best [player] in every sense. He does everything, and he does it every three days. He doesn't just score goals, he scores great goals; each one is better than the last. We are seeing the very best in action."

— *Pep Guardiola, former FC Barcelona player and coach*

Xavi and Iniesta

Soccer games are won with goals, but the team that wins the game is determined by the work of the midfielders. They are the soul of a team, and Barcelona's midfielders have always been among the best, so much that in 2010 all three finalists of the Ballon d'Or were Barcelona players: **Lionel Messi**, Xavi Hernández, and Andrés Iniesta. Just like **Messi**, Xavi and Iniesta are small players full of skill and ball control. They are great at controlling the pace of the game and providing assists to other players. Both Xavi and Iniesta have been World Cup and UEFA Euro champions with the Spanish national team and have helped **Messi** to become the great player he is.

Neymar Jr. and Suárez

After the World Cup in Brazil in 2014, Barcelona decided to create an impressive attacking trident by bringing together the new Brazilian superstar Neymar Jr. and Uruguayan bad boy and mega scorer Luis Suárez to play alongside **Lionel Messi**. Barcelona's decision was made in part in response to rival Real Madrid's impressive striker trio, know as the BBC (for Karim Benzema, Gareth Bale, and Cristiano Ronaldo). Putting together so many megastars doesn't always work, but Barcelona's trio of **Messi**, Neymar Jr., and Suárez ended the season with a whopping 122 goals. **Messi**, by the way, scored 58 of those!

MESSI Quiz #4

Test your knowledge about **Messi**.

Lionel Messi is the FC Barcelona player with the most followers on Facebook, with 79 million fans. The second is Neymar Jr., with 53 million.

Do you know who is third?

a) **Luis Suárez**
b) **Andrés Iniesta**
c) **Ivan Rakitić**
d) **Gerard Piqué**

Find the answer on page 137

FC Barcelona's Facebook page has more than 85 million fans. It is the most followed sports team in the world. Real Madrid has 83 million fans. Do you know which team is in third place?

a) Los Angeles Lakers (NBA)
b) Manchester United FC (Premiere League)
c) Arsenal (Premiere League)
d) Miami Heat (NBA)

ARGENTINA'S
NATIONAL
TEAM

July 2015: Argentina and Chile just finished 120 minutes of intense soccer. This was the final game of Copa América, the oldest soccer tournament in the world and, after the World Cup, the biggest prize in soccer for a South American team. The game was played in Chile, and the host team hoped to win their first Copa América trophy. Argentina really wanted the trophy, too. They had not won the tournament since 1993, and perhaps as important, they hadn't won a major tournament with **Lionel Messi** on the team.

After 90 minutes of play, plus 30 minutes of extra time, the score remained 0–0. Both teams had their chances during the game, particularly Argentina. The albiceleste could have scored in the last minute of the match after a great play by **Messi**, who escaped the determined Chilean defense with his usual combination of quick feet and great vision. The ball got to Argentina striker Gonzalo Higuaín, who missed the chance in a tight angle, and with no time on the clock both teams had to determine the winner in a penalty shoot-out.

"Winning the Copa would round off something spectacular. I really want to win something with the national team."

— *Messi before the Copa América final in 2015*

Messi was the first Argentinian player to take a penalty. **Messi** kicked the ball with great pace and close to the left post. Goal by **Messi**! The penalty shoot-out continued. The Chilean players were perfect, scoring at every turn. The Argentinian players were not as accurate and missed two penalties in a row. Game over. Chile had won the Copa América.

As the Chilean players celebrated, **Messi** sat on the field, covering his face.

Just one year before, Argentina and **Messi** had lost in the 2014 World Cup against Germany. **Messi** and his teammates had two chances to win the most sought-after soccer tournaments for their country. In both competitions, **Messi** had fallen short. His dream to win a major tournament for his home country would have to wait.

10 Years of Lionel Messi Playing for Argentina

Year
Tournament
Result

2005
World Cup U-20 (Netherlands)
Champions
2-1 vs. Nigeria, 2 goals, tournament MVP
and best scorer

Year
Tournament
Result

2006
World Cup (Germany)
Quarterfinals

Year
Tournament
Result

2007
Copa América (Venezuela)
Runners-up

Year
Tournament
Result

2008
Olympic Games (Beijing)
Champions

Year
Tournament
Result

2014
World Cup (Brazil)
Runners-up

Last Major Tournament Won by Argentina
1993 Copa América in Ecuador

The Argentinian national team is one of the most successful teams in soccer. The albiceleste have won the Copa América 14 times, reached five World Cup finals, and won the biggest soccer tournament in the world twice. Their first Word Cup title was in 1978. Playing at home, Argentina beat the Netherlands 3–1 in extra time. The second came in 1986, when Argentina beat Germany 3–2 in the World Cup played in Mexico. The albiceleste were led by Diego Armando Maradona, who played a remarkable tournament and earned the label of one of the best players in soccer history.

14

Copa América titles

2

World Cup titles

Top Ten Argentinian Players of All Time

Hernán Jorge Crespo

Gabriel Batistuta

Mario Kempes

Daniel Alberto Passarella

Diego Armando Maradona

Alfredo Di Stéfano

Juan Román Riquelme

Javier Zanetti

Javier Mascherano

Lionel Messi

After losing the final in both the 2014 World Cup and the 2015 Copa América, many Argentinian fans were upset and critical of **Messi**. When would **Messi** win a tournament for them? All the trophies and records with Barcelona were fine, but Argentinians want him to win with Argentina.

Nobody expects that a single player can win a trophy for the team. Soccer is, after all, a team sport. But many believe that while Maradona had led his country to win the 1986 World Cup, **Messi** has failed to do the same.

Can Messi deliver Argentina a third World Cup trophy?

Only time will tell...

Five Great Players Who Never Won a World Cup

Johan Cruyff *(Netherlands)*
Three-time winner of the Ballon d'Or
World Cups played 1, finals 1

Michel Platini *(France)*
Three-time winner of the Ballon d'Or
World Cups played 3, finals 0

Ferenc Puskás *(Hungary)*
World Cups played 2, finals 1

Paolo Maldini *(Italy)*
World Cups played 4, finals 1

Zico *(Brazil)*
World Cups played 3, finals 0

Four Great Active Players Without a World Cup Title

Lionel Messi *(Argentina)*
World Cups played to date 3, finals to date 1

Cristiano Ronaldo *(Portugal)*
World Cups played to date 3, finals to date 0

Zlatan Ibrahimović *(Sweden)*
World Cups played to date 2, finals to date 0

Arjen Robben *(Netherlands)*
World Cups played to date 3, finals to date 1

The shortage of major trophies with the albiceleste doesn't mean that **Messi** has not given Argentinian fans some fantastic triumphs. In 2005, Argentina won the World Youth Championship (today called World Cup U-20, since players are under 20 years of age) in the Netherlands. In the final match against Nigeria, **Messi** scored two goals and won both the Golden Boot as best goal scorer of the tournament (6 goals) and the Golden Ball as the best player of the tournament.

Three years later, at the Beijing Olympic Games, **Messi** and Argentina won the gold medal in soccer. **Messi** scored two goals in the games and gave teammate Ángel Di María the assist for the winning goal in the final.

Messi's Top Ten Achievements with Argentina

Most goals scored in a year with the national team:
12 goals (shared with Gabriel Batistuta)

Youngest player to score a goal at the World Cup:
18 years and 357 days old (in 2006 vs Serbia and Montenegro)

Most goals scored in all U-20 International competitions (2004–2005):
11 goals (shared with Javier Saviola)

Most goals scored in one FIFA World Cup qualification (2014): 10

Copa América Young Player of the Tournament: 2007

Copa América Top Assist Provider: 2011, 2015

FIFA World Youth Championship Golden Ball: 2005

FIFA World Youth Championship Golden Boot: 2005

MESSI Quiz #5

Test your knowledge about **Messi**.

During his time at Newell's Old Boys, **Messi** was late to an important game.

Do you know why he didn't make it on time?

a) **Messi** couldn't find his cleats
b) **Messi** thought the game was on a different field
c) **Messi** got locked in the bathroom
d) **Messi** thought he could win the game playing only a few minutes

Find the answer on page 137

THE FUTURE

The Future

Many people wonder what will happen with **Messi** in the future. But this is not an easy question to answer. Is he going to stay with Barcelona for the rest of his career? Well, we have to wait and see. Many of the most important soccer teams in the world want to bring him into their ranks and are ready to offer him a very good contract for his many talents. Will he win a World Cup for Argentina? Maybe. If everything goes well, **Messi** will have at least one more chance to lift the biggest soccer trophy in 2018 in Russia. How many more records will he break? If **Messi** stays healthy (away from injuries) he has the potential to break many more records. All these are great questions. But perhaps the most important one is this: How many more times will we be amazed by seeing him on the field, dribbling defenders left and right to finish one more remarkable play with an extraordinary goal. Hopefully, many more times.

Messi and his partner Antonella have two kids: Thiago (born 2012) and Mateo (born 2015).

10,000 Hours
of Soccer

If you are like the millions of kids around the world who dream of being the next **Lionel Messi**, there is bad news and good news. The bad news is that being as good as **Messi** is very, very hard. The good news is that it's not impossible to become a professional soccer player, and being a great one—perhaps as good as **Messi**—can always be your goal.

Messi, of course, has a natural talent for soccer. In other words, he was born for the game. Maybe you are also a natural. But that is not enough. Some experts believe that to become really good at something like playing the piano, spelling, or scoring goals, you have to follow the 10,000 hours rule. In other words you have to practice, practice, and practice some more.

So, do what **Messi** and many soccer players did when they were kids.

Get your soccer ball and get out of the house. Now!

Bring your soccer ball to the park, the gym, parties, and school. Play in the snow, on smooth grassy fields, on bumpy trails in the woods, and on the beach.

Kick it, juggle with it, dribble, and try a fancy trick. Kick it again, juggle again, dribble a bit more, and try another trick.

Find a friend and play.
Invite another friend and play again.

Have fun. Have fun.

And have some more fun!

Be a Superstar!

Dream big.

Play fair and often.

Be yourself.

Love the game.

In the best-case scenario, you may be the next great soccer superstar.

In the worst-case scenario, you will spend endless hours playing the beautiful game.

Not bad.

Glossary

agile — Able to move quickly and lightly.

Ballon d'Or — The biggest award given to the best soccer player every year.

Bundesliga — The top professional soccer league in Germany.

Clásico / Derbi — An old rivalry between two teams from the same league or region.

Copa del Rey — Yearly competition between teams from different divisions in Spain.

Copa Libertadores — An annual soccer tournament where the best clubs of Latin America face each other.

dribble — To skillfully move the ball by repeated taps or kicks.

FIFA — Fédération Internationale de Football Association; the organization that manages soccer all over the world.

FIFA Club World Cup — An annual soccer tournament where the clubs from different regions of the world face each other.

FIFA World Cup — The biggest soccer tournament in the world for national teams. It is played every four years.

FIFA World Youth Championship — The biggest soccer tournament in the world for national teams with players between the ages of 17 and 23.

friendlies — Games played by two teams as preparation for a tournament or competition.

hat trick — When a player scores three goals in the same game.

header — When a player connects with the ball with his/her head.

hormone — Chemical substance necessary for the regular development of our bodies.

Italian Serie A	The top professional soccer league in Italy.
juggle	To control the ball in the air with different parts of the body, such as the feet, knees, or head.
kit	The team's uniform.
La Liga	The top professional soccer league in Spain.
penalty	A free kick awarded to a team when a foul is committed in the penalty area.
striker	A player in the front of the formation whose job is to score goals. Also called a forward.
UEFA	The Union of European Football Associations; UEFA organizes all of the regional soccer clubs and national teams located in Europe.
UEFA Champions League	Also known as the Champions League, this is an annual soccer club competition organized by UEFA.

Answers to Quizzes

Quiz #1:   *a) 2 goals*
Quiz #2:   *c) 3 goals in one game*
Quiz #3:   *c) Red and blue horizontal stripes*
Quiz #4:   *d) Gerard Piqué, with more than 10 million followers; and*
          b) Manchester United FC, with 65 million followers
Quiz #5:   *c) He had to break the bathroom door to get to the game*

More About Messi and Soccer

Books

Messi (World Soccer Legends)
Abbeville Press, Second Edition 2015

Messi: El chico que siempre llegaba tarde y hoy es el primero
Leonardo Faccio
Vintage Español, 2011

Messi, Neymar, Ronaldo
Luca Caioli
Icon Books LTD, 2014

Messi: Un genio en la escuela del Fútbol
Ramiro Martin
Ediciones Lectio, 2013

Index